POPULAR PIANO SOLOS

Pop Hits, Broadway, Movies and More!

ISBN 978-1-4234-0904-5

WILLIS MUSIC

EXCLUSIVELY DISTRIBUTED BY

HAL•LEONARD®

7777 W. BLUEMOUND RD. P.O. BOX 13819 MILWAUKEE, WI 53213

Visit Hal Leonard Online at
www.halleonard.com

Contents

You'll Be in My Heart

from Walt Disney Pictures' TARZAN ™

Use with John Thompson's Modern Course for the Piano FIRST GRADE BOOK, after page 6.

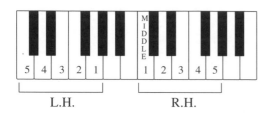

Words and Music by
Phil Collins

With enthusiasm!

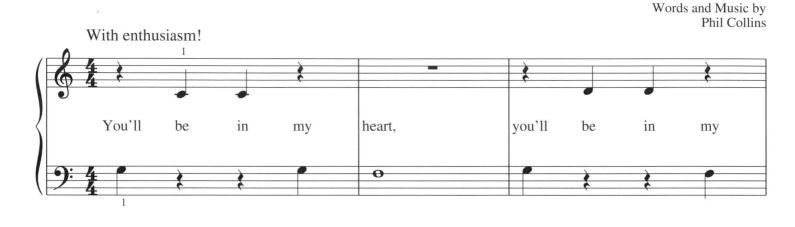

You'll be in my heart, you'll be in my

4

heart from this day on, now and for - ev - er -

Accompaniment (Student plays two octaves higher than written.)

With enthusiasm!

4

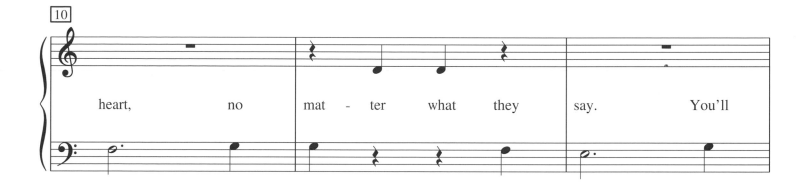

Love Me Tender

Use after page 12.

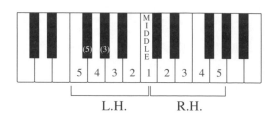

Words and Music by Elvis Presley
and Vera Matson

Not too fast

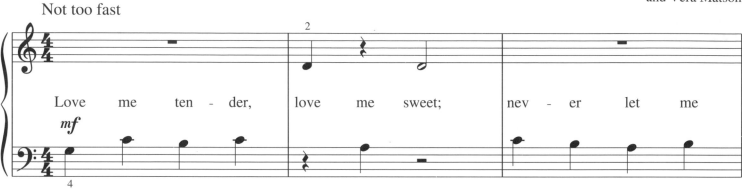

Love me ten - der, love me sweet; nev - er let me

go. You have made my life com - plete,

Accompaniment (Student plays one octave higher than written.)

Not too fast

7

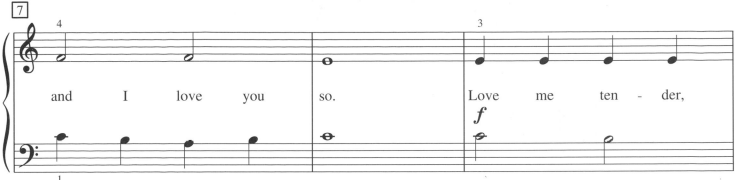

It's a Small World

from "it's a small world" at Disneyland Park and Magic Kingdom Park

Use after page 15.

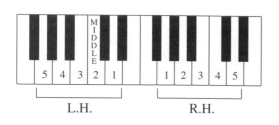

Words and Music by Richard M. Sherman
and Robert B. Sherman

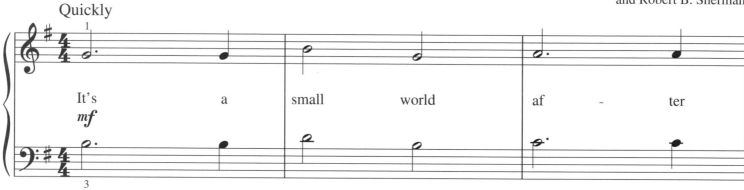

Quickly

It's   a   small   world   af - ter

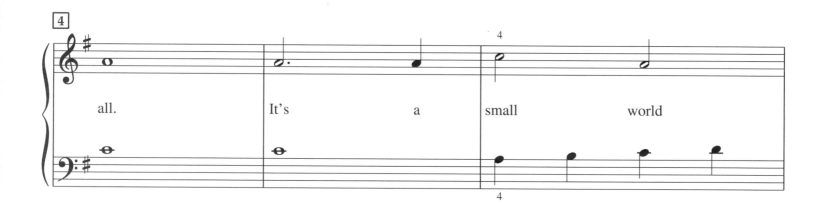

all.   It's   a   small   world

Accompaniment (Student plays one octave higher than written.)

Quickly

af - ter all. It's a

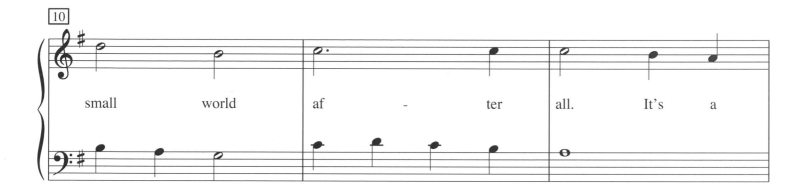

small world af - ter all. It's a

small, small world. _____

1

Edelweiss

from THE SOUND OF MUSIC

Use after page 25.

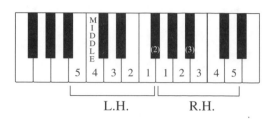

Lyrics by Oscar Hammerstein II
Music by Richard Rodgers

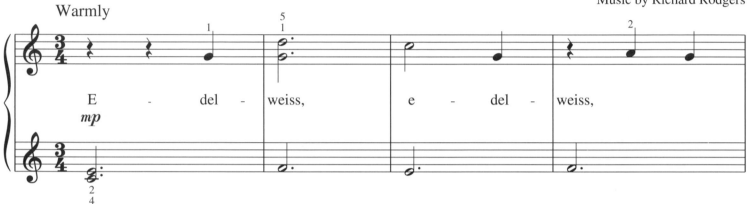

E - del - weiss, e - del - weiss,

ev - 'ry morn - ing you greet me.

Accompaniment (Student plays one octave higher than written.)

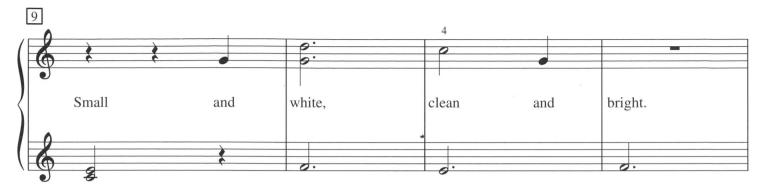

Small and white, clean and bright.

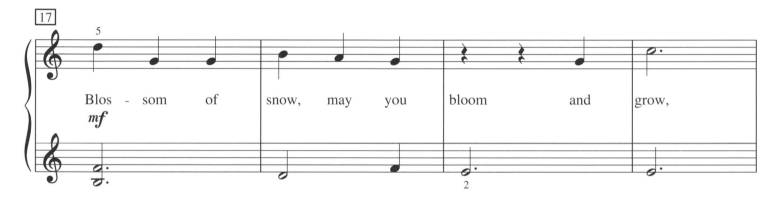

You look hap - py to meet me.

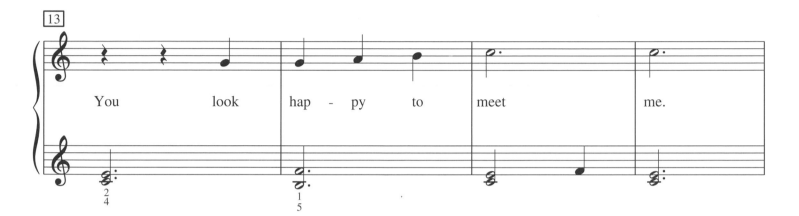

Blos - som of snow, may you bloom and grow,

mf

mp

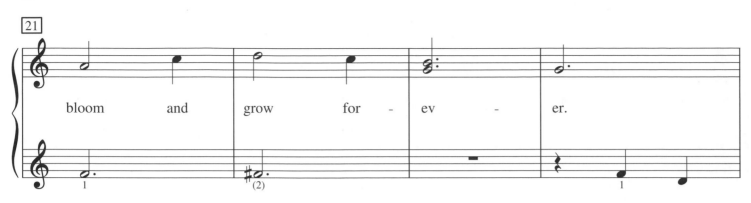

bloom and grow for - ev - er.

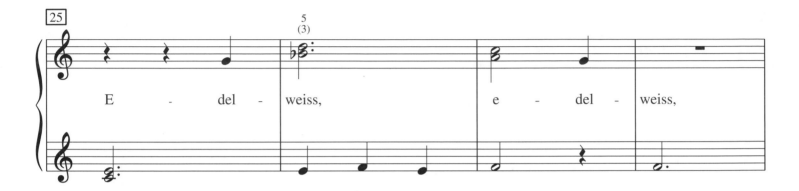

E - del - weiss, e - del - weiss,

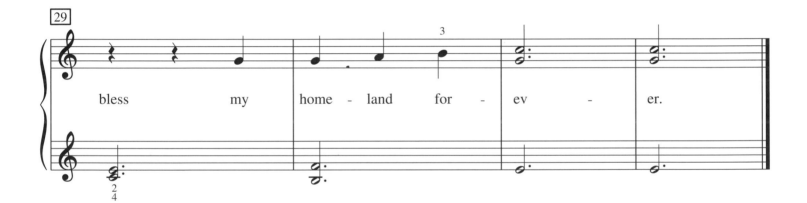

bless my home - land for - ev - er.

Fly Me to the Moon
(In Other Words)

featured in the Motion Picture ONCE AROUND

Use after page 44.

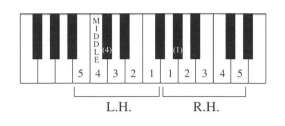

Words and Music by
Bart Howard

Fly me to the moon and let me play a-mong the stars.

Let me see what spring is like on Ju – pi -ter and Mars. In

Accompaniment (Student plays one octave higher than written.)

9
oth - er words, hold my hand! In
13
oth - er words, dar - ling, kiss me!
17
Fill my heart with song and let me sing for - ev - er - more.
f
9
13
17
mf

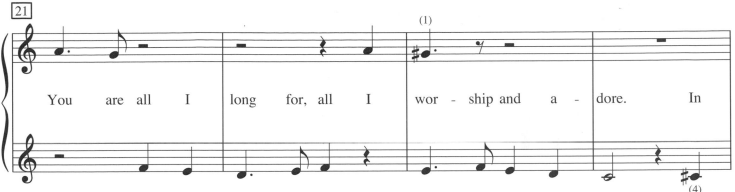

You are all I long for, all I wor - ship and a - dore. In

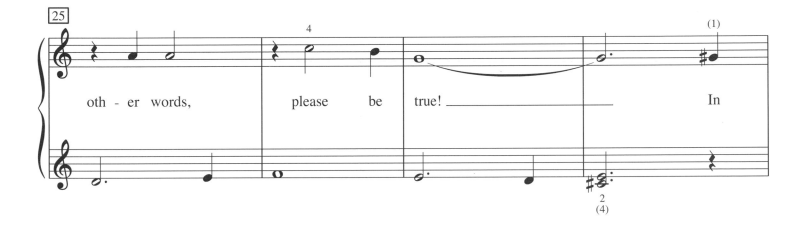

oth - er words, please be true! _____ In

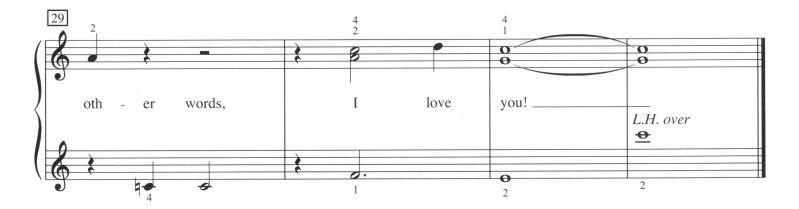

oth - er words, I love you! _____

L.H. over

Oh, What a Beautiful Mornin'

from OKLAHOMA!

Use after page 32.

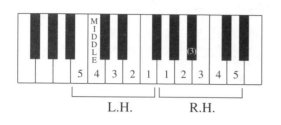

L.H.   R.H.

Lyrics by Oscar Hammerstein II
Music by Richard Rodgers

Cheerfully

Oh,   what   a   beau - ti - ful   morn -

in'.   Oh,   what   a   beau - ti - ful

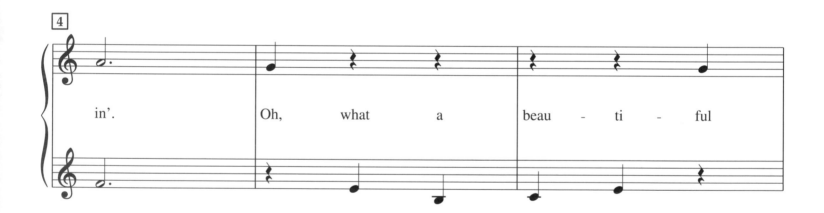

Accompaniment (Student plays one octave higher than written.)

Cheerfully

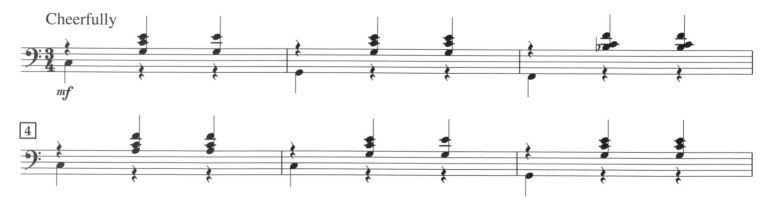

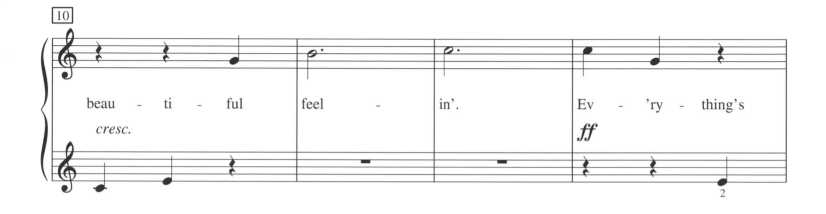

What the World Needs Now Is Love

Use after page 38.

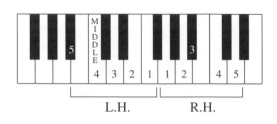

Lyric by Hal David
Music by Burt Bacharach

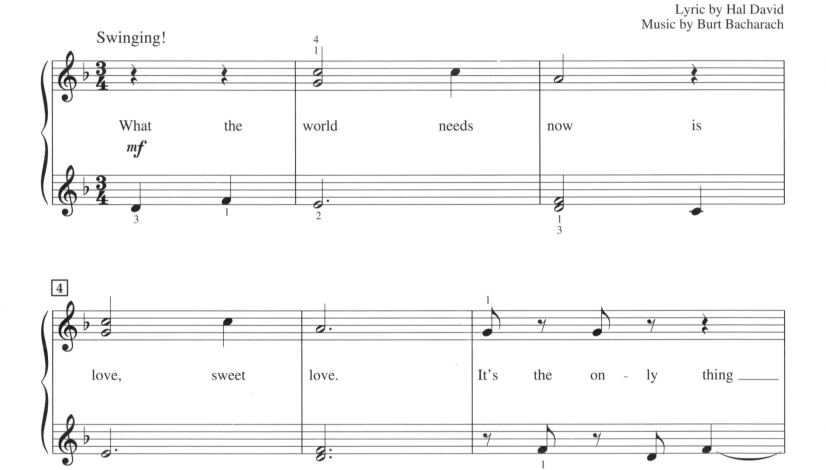

Accompaniment (Student plays one octave higher than written.)

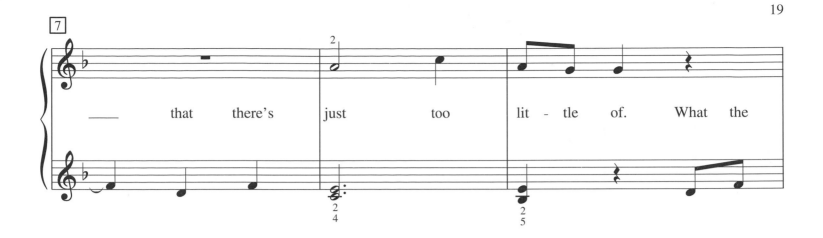

that there's just too lit - tle of. What the

world needs now is love, sweet love.

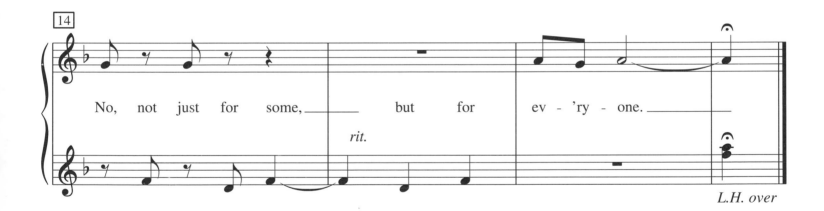

No, not just for some, _____ but for ev - 'ry - one. _____

rit.

L.H. over

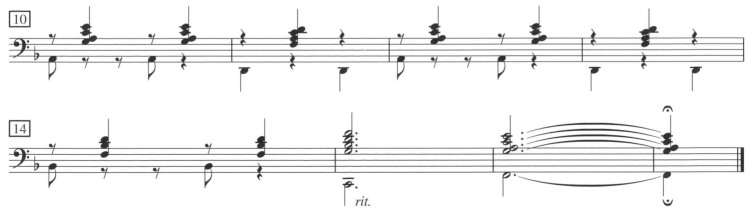

rit.

Let's Go Fly a Kite

from Walt Disney's MARY POPPINS

Use after page 48.

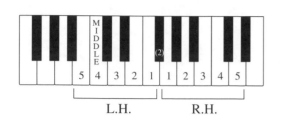

Words and Music by Richard M. Sherman
and Robert B. Sherman

Let's go fly a kite up to the

high-est height! Let's go fly a kite and

Accompaniment (Student plays one octave higher than written.)

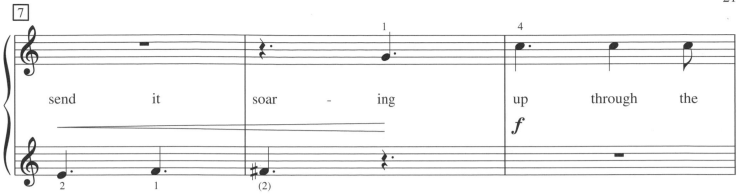

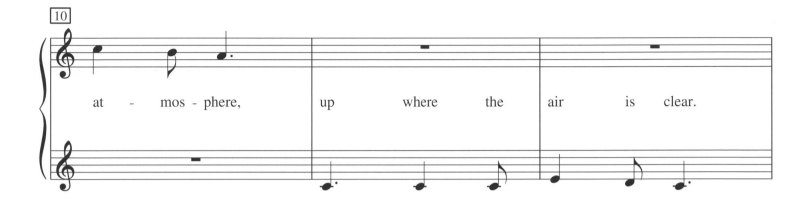

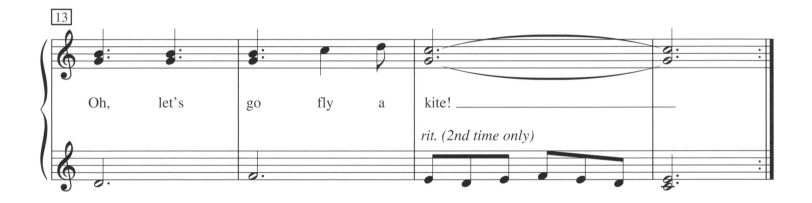

This Is It

Theme from THE BUGS BUNNY SHOW

Use after page 53.

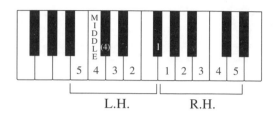

Words and Music by Mack David
and Jerry Livingston

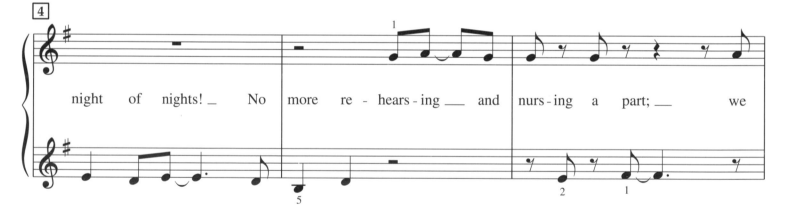

Accompaniment (Student plays one octave higher than written.)

Steadily, at a brisk pace

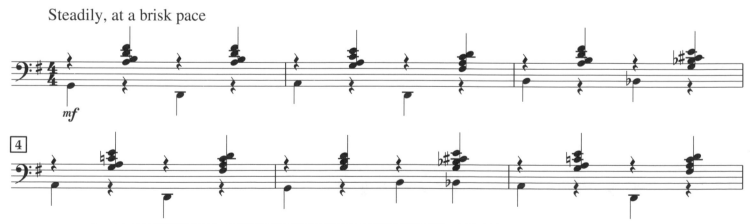

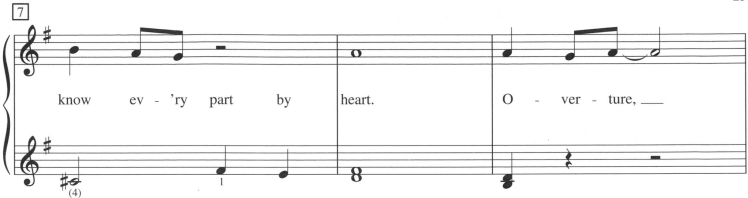

The Rainbow Connection

from THE MUPPET MOVIE

Use after page 50.

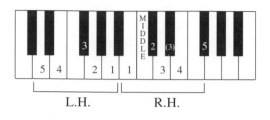

Words and Music by Paul Williams
and Kenneth L. Ascher

Thoughtfully

Why are there so man-y songs a-bout rain-bows, and

what's on the oth - er side? _____

Accompaniment (Student plays two octaves higher than written.)

Thoughtfully

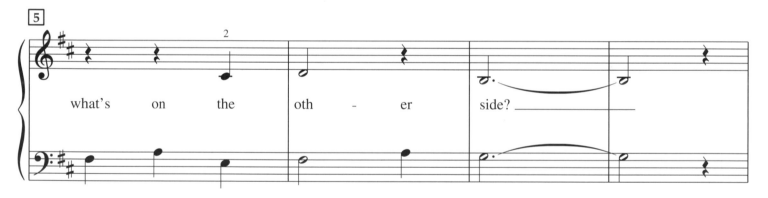

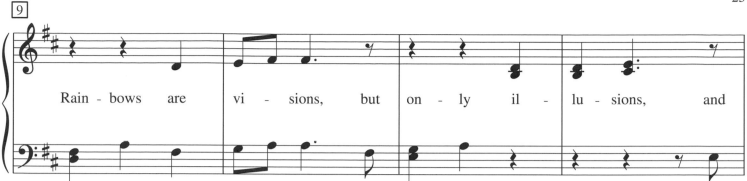

Rain - bows are vi - sions, but on - ly il - lu - sions, and

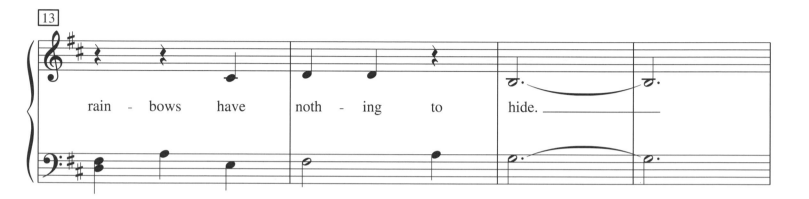

rain - bows have noth - ing to hide. _____

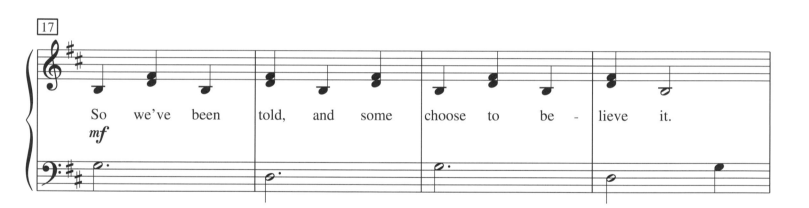

So we've been told, and some choose to be - lieve it.

mf

mp

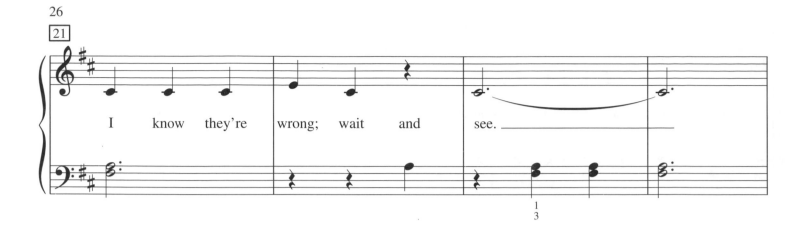

I know they're wrong; wait and see. _____

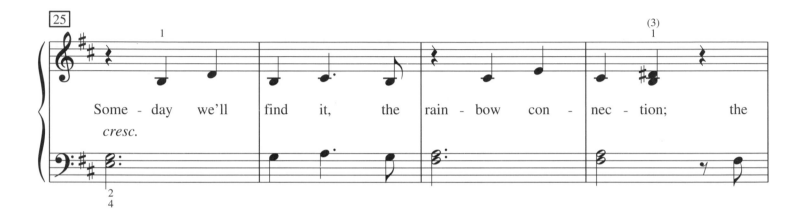

Some - day we'll find it, the rain - bow con - nec - tion; the

cresc.

lov - ers, the dream - ers, and me. _____

cresc.

You Are My Sunshine

Use after page 71.

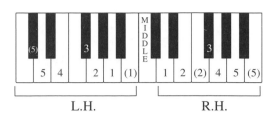

L.H.   R.H.

Words and Music by
Jimmie Davis

Sweetly

You are my sun - shine, _____ my on - ly sun - shine. _____ You make me

hap - py _____ when skies are gray. _____ You'll nev - er

know, dear, _____ how much I love you. Please don't

take my sun - shine a - way. **1.** You are my **2.** way. *rit.*

Go the Distance
(Pop Version)
from Walt Disney Pictures' HERCULES

Use after page 74.

Music by Alan Menken
Lyrics by David Zippel

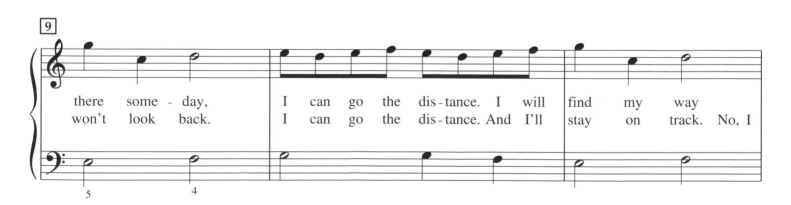

if I can be strong. I know ev - 'ry mile will be worth my while. When I
won't ac - cept de - feat. It's an up - hill slope, but I

go the dis - tance, I'll be right where I be - long.

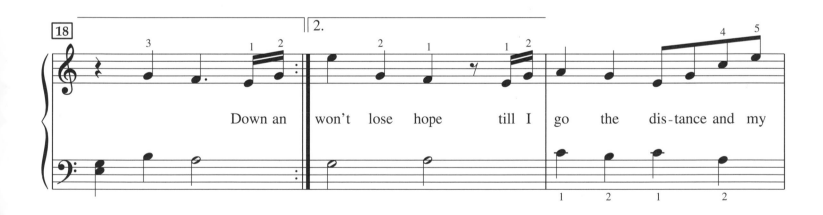

Down an won't lose hope till I go the dis - tance and my

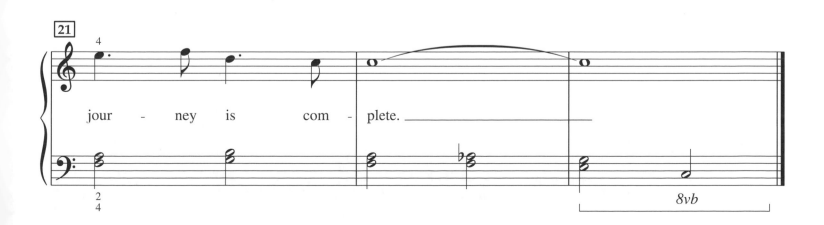

jour - ney is com - plete.

CLASSICAL PIANO SOLOS

Original Keyboard Pieces from Baroque to the 20th Century

Compiled and edited by Philip Low, Sonya Schumann, and Charmaine Siagian

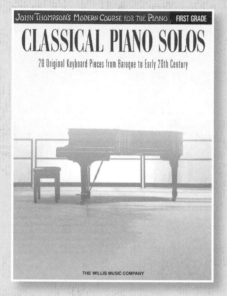

JOHN THOMPSON'S MODERN COURSE FOR THE PIANO / FIRST GRADE

CLASSICAL PIANO SOLOS

20 Original Keyboard Pieces from Baroque to Early 20th Century

THE WILLIS MUSIC COMPANY

First Grade

22 pieces: *Bartók*: A Conversation • *Mélanie Bonis*: Miaou! Ronron! • *Burgmüller*: Arabesque • *Handel*: Passepied • *d'Indy*: Two-Finger Partita • *Köhler*: Andantino • *Müller*: Lyric Etude • *Ryba*: Little Invention • *Schytte*: Choral Etude; Springtime • *Türk*: I Feel So Sick and Faint, and more!
00119738 / $6.99

Second Grade

22 pieces: *Bartók*: The Dancing Pig Farmer • *Beethoven*: Ecossaise • *Bonis*: Madrigal • *Burgmüller*: Progress • *Gurlitt*: Etude in C • *Haydn*: Dance in G • *d'Indy*: Three-Finger Partita • *Kirnberger*: Lullaby in F • *Mozart*: Minuet in C • *Petzold*: Minuet in G • *Purcell*: Air in D Minor • *Rebikov*: Limping Witch Lurking • *Schumann*: Little Piece • *Schytte*: A Broken Heart, and more!
00119739 / $6.99

Third Grade

20 pieces: *CPE Bach*: Presto in C Minor • *Bach/Siloti*: Prelude in G • *Burgmüller*: Ballade • *Cécile Chaminade*: Pièce Romantique • *Dandrieu*: The Fifers • *Gurlitt*: Scherzo in D Minor • *Hook*: Rondo in F • *Krieger*: Fantasia in C • *Kullak*: Once Upon a Time • *MacDowell*: Alla Tarantella • *Mozart*: Rondino in D • *Rebikov*: Playing Soldiers • *Scarlatti*: Sonata in G • *Schubert*: Waltz in F Minor, and more!
00119740 / $7.99

Fourth Grade

18 pieces: *CPE Bach*: Scherzo in G • *Teresa Carreño*: Berceuse • *Chopin*: Prelude in E Minor • *Gade*: Little Girls' Dance • *Granados*: Valse Poetic No. 6 • *Grieg*: Arietta • *Handel*: Prelude in G • *Heller*: Sailor's Song • *Kuhlau*: Sonatina in C • *Kullak*: Ghost in the Fireplace • *Moszkowski*: Tarentelle • *Mozart*: Allegro in G Minor • *Rebikov*: Music Lesson • *Satie*: Gymnopedie No. 1 • *Scarlatti*: Sonata in G • *Telemann*: Fantasie in C, and more!
00119741 / $7.99

Fifth Grade

19 pieces: *Bach*: Prelude in C-sharp Major • *Beethoven*: Moonlight sonata • *Chopin*: Waltz in A-flat • *Cimarosa*: Sonata in E-flat • *Coleridge-Taylor*: They Will Not Lend Me a Child • *Debussy*: Doctor Gradus • *Grieg*: Troldtog • *Griffes*: Lake at Evening • *Lyadov*: Prelude in B Minor • *Mozart*: Fantasie in D Minor • *Rachmaninoff*: Prelude in C-sharp Minor • *Rameau*: Les niais de Sologne • *Schumann*: Farewell • *Scriabin*: Prelude in D, and more!
00119742 / $8.99

The *Classical Piano Solos* series offers carefully-leveled, original piano works from Baroque to the early 20th century, featuring the simplest classics in Grade 1 to concert-hall repertoire in Grade 5. An assortment of pieces are featured, including familiar masterpieces by Bach, Beethoven, Mozart, Grieg, Schumann, and Bartók, as well as several lesser-known works by composers such as Melanie Bonis, Anatoly Lyadov, Enrique Granados, Vincent d'Indy, Theodor Kullak, and Samuel Coleridge-Taylor.

• Grades 1-4 are presented in a suggested order of study. Grade 5 is laid out chronologically.

• Features clean, easy-to-read engravings with clear but minimal editorial markings.

• View complete repertoire lists of each book along with sample music pages at **www.willispianomusic.com**.

The series was compiled to loosely correlate with the *John Thompson Modern Course*, but can be used with any method or teaching situation.

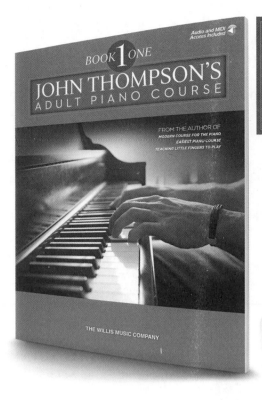

REDISCOVER
JOHN THOMPSON'S
ADULT PIANO COURSE

ADULT PIANO COURSE

Recently re-engraved and updated, *John Thompson's Adult Piano Course* was compiled with the mature student in mind. Adults have the same musical road to travel as the younger student, but the study material for mature students will differ slightly in content. Since these beloved books were written and arranged especially for adults, they contain a wonderful mix of classical arrangements, well-known folk-tunes and outstanding originals that many will find a pleasure to learn and play. Most importantly, the student is always encouraged to play as artistically and with as much musical understanding as possible. Access to orchestrations online is available and features two tracks for each piece: a demo track with the piano part, and one with just the accompaniment.

00122297	Book 1 – Book/Online Audio	$14.99
00412639	Book 1 – Book Only	$6.99
00122300	Book 2 – Book/Online Audio	$14.99
00415763	Book 2 – Book Only	$6.99

POPULAR PIANO SOLOS – JOHN THOMPSON'S ADULT PIANO COURSE

12 great arrangements that can be used on their own, or as a supplement to *John Thompson's Adult Piano Course.*
Each book includes access to audio tracks online that be downloaded or streamed.

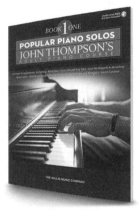

BOOK 1
arr. Carolyn Miller
Born Free • Can't Help Falling in Love • Every Breath You Take • Fields of Gold • Give My Regards to Broadway • A Groovy Kind of Love • My Life • Ob-La-Di, Ob-La-Da • Open Arms • Raindrops Keep Fallin' on My Head • Rainy Days and Mondays • Sweet Caroline.

00124215 Book/Online Audio $12.99

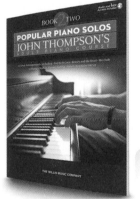

BOOK 2
arr. Eric Baumgartner & Glenda Austin
And So It Goes • Beauty and the Beast • Getting to Know You • Hey Jude • If My Friends Could See Me Now • Lollipop • My Favorite Things • Nadia's Theme • Strawberry Fields Forever • Sunrise, Sunset • Sway (Quien Será) • You Raise Me Up.

00124216 Book/Online Audio $12.99

Also Available, JOHN THOMPSON RECITAL SERIES:

SPIRITUALS
Intermediate to Advanced Level
Six excellent arrangements that are ideal for recital or church service. Titles: Deep River • Heav'n, Heav'n • I Want to Be Ready (Walk in Jerusalem, Jus' like John) • Nobody Knows De Trouble I've Seen • Short'nin' Bread • Swing Low, Sweet Chariot.

00137218 .... $6.99

THEME AND VARIATIONS
Intermediate to Advanced Level
Fantastic recital variations that are sure to impress: Chopsticks • Variations on Mary Had a Little Lamb • Variations on Chopin's C Minor Prelude • Three Blind Mice - Variations on the Theme • Variations on Twinkle, Twinkle, Little Star.

00137219.. $8.99

WALTZES
Intermediate to Advanced Level
Excellent, virtuosic arrangements of famous romantic waltzes: Artist's Life (Strauss) • Paraphrase on the Beautiful Blue Danube (Strauss) • Dark Eyes (Russian Cabaret Song) • Vienna Life (Strauss) • Waltz of the Flowers (Tchaikovsky) • Wedding of the Winds (John T. Hall).

00137220.. $8.99

Prices, contents, and availability subject to change without notice.

CLASSIC PIANO REPERTOIRE

The *Classic Piano Repertoire* series includes popular as well as lesser-known pieces from a select group of composers out of the Willis piano archives. Every piece has been newly engraved and edited with the aim to preserve each composer's original intent and musical purpose.

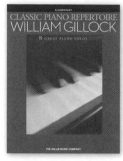

WILLIAM GILLOCK – ELEMENTARY
8 Great Piano Solos
Dance in Ancient Style • Little Flower Girl of Paris • On a Paris Boulevard • Rocking Chair Blues • Sliding in the Snow • Spooky Footsteps • A Stately Sarabande • Stormy Weather.
00416957 ....$8.99

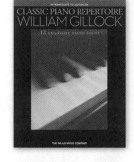

WILLIAM GILLOCK – INTERMEDIATE TO ADVANCED
12 Exquisite Piano Solos
Classic Carnival • Etude in A Major (The Coral Sea) • Etude in E Minor • Etude in G Major (Toboggan Ride) • Festive Piece • A Memory of Vienna • Nocturne • Polynesian Nocturne • Sonatina in Classic Style • Sonatine • Sunset • Valse Etude.
00416912 .... $12.99

EDNA MAE BURNAM – ELEMENTARY
8 Great Piano Solos
The Clock That Stopped • The Friendly Spider • A Haunted House • New Shoes • The Ride of Paul Revere • The Singing Cello • The Singing Mermaid • Two Birds in a Tree.
00110228 ....$8.99

EDNA MAE BURNAM – INTERMEDIATE TO ADVANCED
13 Memorable Piano Solos
Butterfly Time • Echoes of Gypsies • Hawaiian Leis • Jubilee! • Longing for Scotland • Lovely Senorita • The Mighty Amazon River • Rumbling Rumba • The Singing Fountain • Song of the Prairie • Storm in the Night • Tempo Tarantelle • The White Cliffs of Dover.
00110229 .... $12.99

JOHN THOMPSON – ELEMENTARY
9 Great Piano Solos
Captain Kidd • Drowsy Moon • Dutch Dance • Forest Dawn • Humoresque • Southern Shuffle • Tiptoe • Toy Ships • Up in the Air.
00111968 ....$8.99

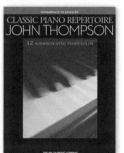

JOHN THOMPSON – INTERMEDIATE TO ADVANCED
12 Masterful Piano Solos
Andantino (from Concerto in D Minor) • The Coquette • The Faun • The Juggler • Lagoon • Lofty Peaks • Nocturne • Rhapsody Hongroise • Scherzando in G Major • Tango Carioca • Valse Burlesque • Valse Chromatique.
00111969 .... $12.99

LYNN FREEMAN OLSON – EARLY TO LATER ELEMENTARY
14 Great Piano Solos
Caravan • Carillon • Come Out! Come Out! (Wherever You Are) • Halloween Dance • Johnny, Get Your Hair Cut! • Jumping the Hurdles • Monkey on a Stick • Peter the Pumpkin Eater • Pony Running Free • Silent Shadows • The Sunshine Song • Tall Pagoda • Tubas and Trumpets • Winter's Chocolatier.
00294722 ....$9.99

LYNN FREEMAN OLSON – EARLY TO MID-INTERMEDIATE
13 Distinctive Piano Solos
Band Wagon • Brazilian Holiday • Cloud Paintings • Fanfare • The Flying Ship • Heroic Event • In 1492 • Italian Street Singer • Mexican Serenade • Pageant Dance • Rather Blue • Theme and Variations • Whirlwind.
00294720 ....$9.99

CLOSER LOOK View sample pages and hear audio excerpts online at **www.halleonard.com**

www.willispianomusic.com

www.facebook.com/willispianomusic

Prices, content, and availability subject to change without notice.